Cathedral of Nervous Horses

CATHEDRAL OF NERVOUS HORSES

W. E. Butts

The Hobblebush Granite State Poetry Series, Volume IV
HOBBLEBUSH BOOKS
Brookline, New Hampshire

Copyright © 2012 by W. E. Butts

All rights reserved. No part of this work may be used or reproduced in any manner whatsoever without written permission from the publisher, except in the case of brief quotations embodied in critical articles and reviews.

Composed in Adobe Arno Pro at Hobblebush Books

Printed in the United States of America

Cover: Giovanni Battista Tiepolo, *Triumph of Hercules*, c. 1761, The Currier Museum of Art, Manchester, New Hampshire Museum Purchase: Currier Funds, 1959.10

Author photograph by S Stephanie

ISBN: 978-0-9845921-7-3

Library of Congress Control Number: 2012938922

The Hobblebush Granite State Poetry Series, Volume IV
Editors: Sidney Hall Jr. and Rodger Martin

HOBBLEBUSH BOOKS
17-A Old Milford Road
Brookline, New Hampshire 03033
www.hobblebush.com

*For Keith A. Kuzmak,
and for my father, Russell
and mother, Ruth*

Contents

FROM *THE REQUIRED DANCE* (1990)

The Inheritance   3
Silver Lake   4
The Canal   5
The Funeral   6
What We Did Wrong, 1956   8
The Last Hold   9
The Balance   11
Martin's Nursing Home   13
From the Cabin at Otter Lake   14
The Vacant Lot on Jefferson Avenue   15
How We Pray   16
Poem for Richard Hugo   17

UNCOLLECTED POEMS (1982–1995)

First Catch   21
Remembering What Was Said   22
Anatomy Lesson   23
Murder at Jug City   25
Day Labor   26
In the Woods at Hills Acres   27
Desire   28
Early Evening at Marginal Way   30
The Gathering   31

FROM *MOVIES IN A SMALL TOWN* (1997)

The Commuter   35
Lost   37
Solitude   38
Appearances   39
Florida   40
Chloe's Epistemology   41
Father's Shirt   42
Meditations on My Fiftieth Birthday   43
I Thought of the Clouded, Moonless Night   44

    The River   45
    1948   47
    The Note   48
    The Lover   49
    Movies in a Small Town, 1957   50

FROM *SUNDAY EVENING AT THE STARDUST CAFÉ* (2006)

    Innocence   53
    1954: Two Parades   55
    Black Squirrels   56
    Sunday Evening at the Stardust Café   58
    All Our Quick Days   60
    City That Never Sleeps   62
    The Question   63
    Eight Ball   65
    Particular Hearts   67
    The Station   68
    Selling the Church   70
    My Father's Name   71
    Sunday Factory   72
    Red Jack   73
    The Train   74

FROM *RADIO TIME* (2011)

    Porcelain   79
    Art Lesson   81
    Apples   83
    The Gift of Unwanted Knowledge   84
    The Calling   86
    Odds Against Tomorrow   87
    Our Fathers' Clothes   89
    Radio Time   90
    The Other Language   91
    The Industrial Diamonds of 1964   93
    The Annual Richard Milhous Nixon Pig Roast &
        4th of July Celebration   94
    At the Currier Gallery of Art   95
    Everywhere is Everywhere   96
    Against Happiness   97

What to Say if the Birds Ask   98
The Garden   99
Thrush & Squirrel   100

NEW POEMS

Absence & Event   103
Wonder   105
At The Wilkes-Barre/Scranton Airport Meditation Room   106
Brotherhood   107
Ash   108
Who Can Say?   109
Mise-en-scène   110
The Past   112

Notes   113
Acknowledgments   115

FROM *THE REQUIRED DANCE* (1990)

The Inheritance

I was eight when my uncle died.
A year later, my parents and I
buried the family dog in our back yard,
by a patch of lilies-of-the-valley.
I was always conscious
of stepping over those bones,
but it was not for ten years,
the day I found my father fallen
on the floor, too weak
to climb into his bed,
that I was finally afraid.

I watched him at the hospital,
his frail body curled
like a fetus, and realized
he was going back, and I wanted
to take hold of those shrunken hands
and lead him there myself.

When his breath left him, my mother's eyes shut.
The geography of her life became
a small, hard planet spinning inside her.
Galaxies collapsed, worlds were thrown
from their arcs, her hands went limp,
stars exploded, constellations were rearranged
and I understood, I was now the man she loved.

Silver Lake

The first time I saw it, I was
five years old, and every day
there the sun exploded
into bright red strawberries.
Mother fed us with sweet milk,
while Father swam the cool morning.

Afternoons, I would walk along
the shore, stop and bend to the glitter
of the lake, as he stood, just
close enough in the white sand.

Our summer trips to the cottage
always began with a slow drive
in Uncle's '49 gray Pontiac.
Year after year, at the end
of vacation, he returned
to bring us home. We went,
not sure that's what we wanted.

I live in a city I didn't know
about then. My father and uncle
are both dead. Mother writes
often from the nursing home,
and I remember the shine of trout
beneath circling pools.

The Canal

My daughter and I sit on a bank
by the canal where, a hundred years
ago, my great uncle drove barge.
We have walked through tall grass,
weed and disordered wood to come here.
Together, we select small, flat stones
to skip across the water.
For a while, we watch their brief lives
leap and disappear. Then we make a game.
I toss a stone that creates a ring
over the surface. She tries to throw
hers within its center. She notices
the circles cross one another.
I am reminded of cells in the body,
and how each precisely duplicates
its elements. We return
to the dense, difficult path. Beneath
our concentric circles, stones sink
like the dead into their graves.

The Funeral

Father has been buried here
half my life. Next to him
is a grave for me. At his other side
my mother lies this morning,
beneath incense and Latin chants.
In this Catholic cemetery
named St. Francis, I think
of parochial school. Counting beads
gave children license to be
cruel as thorns, and faith
that weddings, eating flesh,
and funerals were, after all,
the same. There are no saints.
The last angel has flown into
a dark eye, and will not return.
It begins to rain. Mother, we look
at your grave and see an end.
My daughter has your jewelry.
The ceremony isn't right. There
should be a way to keep you
out of death. A photograph
of you and Father shows
what your life was like.
In 1942 you wore a beaded dress,
and smiled. Father stood
beside an elm, and knew this day
was good. Next autumn
you were married, two years
before my birth. You held
those events as sacraments,
even after death and loss.

Now, in an uneventful town,
left smaller by your leaving,
the rain comes harder as we move
away and home, wherever that may be.

What We Did Wrong, 1956

What we thought we did wrong was lust
for the new bodies of the older girls.
We delighted in a child's tests of cruelty.
Tearing things apart made us whole.
The Jewish junkman suspected this,
and drove his old gray daily by us
in silence. The time he left his wagon
unattended, we set fire to the oily rags
piled up in it. When he came screaming
down the road, the air blackened
with our laughter. We laughed at the
yellow-eyed Negro who chased us epileptic
through the town's main street,
on Saturday afternoons when we were twelve.
And we made the alcoholic Indian dance
around the flagpole, in front
of the post office, until the night
he was run over dead by a drunken
traveling salesman on 490. Twenty-five years
later, I see those older girls young
and feel again that dumb ache
after a madness none of us understood.

The Last Hold

We found him sweeping the streets
of a downtown Italian market,
and drove him home with us,
to the side of a dirt road.
He had been the city's favorite derelict—
fifty-six years old, unkempt gray hair,
beard, a paralyzed hand, and he wore
the same pair of pants
throughout the year I knew him.
His name was James, he would insist,
and if you called him "Jimmy,"
he wouldn't speak to you for a week.
When he got angry, he waved his bad hand.
He told us, "Desire deferred
sickens the heart," and declared
the greatest day in American history
was when "the lights went out
in New York City and youth directed
traffic with their white handkerchiefs."
Once, he tried to burn down a field,
but again and again the wind
put out the match flame. He slept
with the dogs, who knew him best,
and often woke, cried with them
in the darkness, and recalled a time
when, living in a Catholic worker's home,
he entered a cathedral in a drunken rage,
removed the icons he discovered there,
and threw them over a cliff. After he moved

away, I stood alone in the empty room
that had been his, and felt a constriction
at the base of my skull, where something had
reached up to take one, last, desperate hold.

The Balance

I am visiting someone in an apartment
located around the corner
from a long row of broken-down tenements.
At either end of that block
is a liquor store. We have little money,
but in celebration of my return
from New York City to Boston,
we roll two dollars worth of pennies,
and go to one of the liquor stores to buy beer.
The gaunt cashier taps his jeweled,
long-nailed fingers on the counter suspiciously,
picks up a roll, balances it
in his slender palm and says,
"Man, there ain't no fifty cent in here."
He opens the roll, counts the pennies
and he's right—forty-eight.
I envy this ability to know
the full measure of a thing by its weight,
no more—no less.
Between us, we have two pennies.
On the way back, I notice
a disheveled figure sprawled across the steps
of a boarded-up brick building.
I'm told he lives there, has for years.
He's luckier than most.
People give him things, take care of him.
Later, we drink beer and talk
about women we thought loved us once.
I want to say something is terrible and wrong,

that there's more to this evening
than our carefully measured desperation,
then realize, I am at peace
in a friend's home.

MARTIN'S NURSING HOME

Black ladies in pink dresses walk and wheel
the dying into the solarium. A woman,
like someone recalling an adolescent love,
cannot name what she had for dinner,
but insists it was very good. A man points
at a bookcase, and claims he read every book
before he came here, then says, "But that's not
the whole story of my life." There's something
sinister about the way the dusty windows refuse
to allow winter light to enter the room.
This is a place where the old surrender the day
to a bite of forbidden candy, or a long,
heavenly pull from what may be the last cigarette.
Television announces the news above
their bowed heads and the cracked tile floor.
Afternoons, they wait in the cold, grave lobby
for the visitor that never comes, then reminisce
over the children who could have treated them well.
Once a month, there are two glasses of wine
in the basement, and the required dance.

From the Cabin at Otter Lake

Across the frozen lake,
slight wind and evening glare.
The house on the opposite bank
disappears. Tomorrow, it rises
like light. That old man
wearing a red shirt lives alone
in a gray shack. When he dies,
the wood he has cut will become rock.
The lost echo of the saw's drone
will return to the lake.
There are many ways to love.
An armful of ash
along the path to the woodpile
is one.

The Vacant Lot on Jefferson Avenue

The gray and green shingled house
is gone. Gone the magnolia tree
that spread its soft petals
where the dog ran in summer.
Remember the joy in that place.
Remember, too, pain so real
it made us weep honest tears.
We believed in spirits, certain
they were good in some way we wanted.
Poverty taught us need, and care.
Those years were passion, or its lack.
What vague hopes we had then return,
today, in winter. If I stand here
long enough, will I see again
the rooms we once moved through?
On a nearby maple branch, two sparrows
perch, swell and flutter.

How We Pray

We walk through a place
where men sleep in elegant cars,
and voices flutter onto the street
like magnolias across a lawn.
At the Baptist Church, women
sing *Jesus. Jesus. Jesus.*
My three-year-old child
wants to know what those people
are doing. I tell her this
is how we pray, and then
the spirit has faith in its body.
That is why there is dancing.
A hymn demands we go to a mountain.
The gleam of sweating faces
and rhythm of clapping hands
will take us there. Not poverty,
need for grace is what we believe. My daughter,
rich from her mother's country,
doesn't notice her father lives poor,
but understands flowers rise
from the mouths of the forgotten.

Poem for Richard Hugo

I. MONTANA RESCUE MISSION

If we sang the hymns and prayed, we ate
the poor meal. At night, women rose in our sleep
like angels of childhood, children laughed,
and money blessed our palms. When we woke,
no women floated through the dank stench
of rotting mattresses. If children laughed,
they gnashed their teeth and jeered. Any brand
of cigarette was a currency we could believe.
Mornings in the tan air and dust, we sat looking
at the earth which bore us, and tried to think
of simple ways to save our lives. In that alley
behind the blue stucco mission, we knew "Eternity Now"
said there was no hope. Wind from the plains
swirled heat over our failures, and each day
lingered homeless. If mountains mattered,
they pointed a permanent direction to a heaven
we couldn't see. When we sang, our voices cracked.
When we prayed, we didn't mean it.

II. BELIEVING IT IS SO

Believe in a voice of stone,
then listen for its one true sound,
echo of water. Names are what we live by.
Call the world forever.
Believe this is so because
you have made certain it will go on.
Remember the woman who haunts the river?
The sand in your throat is her last song,

and trout run every spring. Summer
in Montana you were dying. I could not
see you. I turned east like a plains Indian
hunting mystic truth. Missoula to Billings
I wandered telling sacred skies, "It's wrong."
Black nights on the prairie, unseen and evil
creatures made their terrible noises. Antelope
soared over fields at dawn, horses
raced through mountain wind, and mothers
fed their sons. We need a spirit
water won't offend, and a covenant:
Be kind. Live your life as if it were
a promise you had to keep, or die.

UNCOLLECTED POEMS (1982–1995)

First Catch

The stars were blinking off
and thick, wet worms
thrilled me as they twisted
between my fingers like separate parts
of the same determined body.
Then father and I walked
through the mist-filled dawn behind the house
to the river.
Father baited the hooks
and cast his line in a long, curved arc,
slow and deliberate as any hawk
I'd seen riding thermals above the hills
on the far bank. I was fascinated
by the stilled, mysterious water.
Somewhere a bullfrog was croaking,
and the reeds and willows stirred.

My line was next.
He taught me how to swing the rod,
and snap my wrist
so I could also make it soar.
We sat down like two men,
to rest and talk, to wait.
A small bass leapt into the brightened air,
its blue and silver flash quivering
like my child's heart.
Father's calm voice floated over me
while I pulled and tugged,
until suddenly this strange and living thing
was shaking at my feet.
We wondered, together, at what we'd done,
and Father watched
as I returned the river's secret.

Remembering What Was Said

We look over the water,
where willows lie rippling.
Under the curve of stone bridge,
the lost echo of my name is silent.
I've brought you, my daughter,
to a dispossessed past:
Grandfather's hardware store gone,
the dining car a fast-food restaurant,
the white clapboard schoolhouse
cleared for a gymnasium.
Across the bank, the house I grew up in
is renovated, and no longer poor.
No sunfish glitter near the surface
of the creek, and my mother lies
dying in a nursing home.

And now, in bright August,
we sit on a park bench in front
of the town hall that has not changed.
A siren suddenly startles the birds
from their branches, and from the hotel
on the corner, white-aproned and large
as I recalled, the owner — bartender
and member of the volunteer fire department—
comes out to the street and directs traffic.
The need for rescue has, at least, remained.

But I wanted to tell you these dreams:
the nightmare of my father's sunken flesh
that first year after his death, how
he returned to my sleep a decade later,
whole and newly living, and said
a single, healing thing.

Anatomy Lesson

We view the da Vinci exhibit, "Anatomy of Man."
I read the four universal conditions:
"joy, weeping, fear and fighting,"
and his theory of a three-sectioned brain,
how the energy of thought passes through intellect,
memory, imagination, then back again.

I am here with my daughter, who's twenty-one,
an artist, and so strikingly beautiful
I am terrified and pleased at once.

When her mother and I just divorced,
and she was five or six, she would visit me with paper
and crayons and draw, over and over,
a female figure in a multi-colored gown,
who had long, curled orange hair,
large, almond eyes, and red upturned lips.
There was never a nose. She said
it was a face that didn't need a nose
because she couldn't make one.

In a painting of an autopsy, I examine
intestines curving inside the cavity
of a blue corpse, like the soul's signature,
and recall that story my father heard
in a barroom: da Vinci, several years
into his work on "The Last Supper,"
frustrated in his search for someone
despicable enough to portray Judas, went
to the dungeons of Milan and discovered him.
During the first sitting, the man fell, sobbing,
"Don't you remember me? I was your Christ."

Later, at the kitchen table, my daughter and I
talk about the interpretation of the brain,
and she draws three circles, each one progressively
diminishing in size toward emptiness,
or imagination—the small release that saves us.

Murder at Jug City

> *In and near this village of 100, four people were murdered between 1922 and 1924. The mystery of the crimes has never been solved. The investigators were satisfied that the same person was responsible, and the killer was a resident of the neighborhood.*
> — ARCH MERRILL, STAGECOACH TOWNS

We can't believe the search won't end,
and the police guess one of us
stole the money hidden in old coffee tins
and cookie jars, took it to town and drank
until the bartender cursed his coin.
Dogs turn weak with winter and line either entrance
to the only street, their yellow milky stares
gone mad. They know. They snarl and bark.
Four dead. There's no way out.
Each of us wonders why he was born here,
and what sin won't let him leave. This life
must be forbidden and should be punished,
how else can we fill the church?
The police were right. Tonight, someone
lies crazed on a cold attic floor,
while another mourns the sister she buried
today, whom she cannot forgive. The lights
in our bedrooms are lit, and windows
shine like the eyes of insomniacs.
The police were wrong. There is that
simple fact about who we are, etched
like an epitaph within the sleep we wait for.

Day Labor

At the hospital, he is directed
through a dark, descending corridor
to a man in a white smock,
colorless eyes, and face the color
of concrete. The task is to gather
what's left of the dead.
He tries to think of anything
except the twisted masses
of interior flesh he carries gently
to the fire. He knows loneliness
is a man in early morning shadow,
standing outside a still closed
labor pool. He places one of the gallon jugs
in a box marked for incineration,
and a brown, vacant eye twists up at him.
Because men and women cannot always live
together in pain, he thinks of his wife
and wants to forget. He has become
a watchman of sorrow, and must do this thing.
When he is finished, he returns
to his rented room and weeps for the dead,
the living, and all their parts.

In the Woods at Hills Acres

In the woods behind the house, leaves
swirl and fold like envelopes,
carrying their brief messages of wind.

For half a century, I've been walking
somewhere. Once, on a crisp afternoon
like this, I entered a clearing

just in time to see a hunter
with his rifle raised and aimed at me,
an instant when not even the chirping

lyric code of sparrows, that insists
we belong to the world, can make the heart
believe it could be at the center of anything,

and I was like one of those creatures
in the forest that seems certainly doomed,
yet somehow trembles through its next breath.

As my lover left this morning
for work, I remembered loneliness—a room in Boston,
traffic angry in the narrow street,

and a man getting off the bus
at Fargo, North Dakota, bewildered
in front of an abandoned train station, years ago.

Desire

Stoned-out boys bump
their skateboards down the steps

in front of the Montpelier City Hall,
as girls stand outside

in feigned disinterest,
and one of the boys skates by

balancing a pole on his forehead,
but I know even this won't work,

that tonight the boys will go home
alone, confused about the girls,

about being born where desire
doesn't matter, although they keep

trying, until they marry the girls
who now turn their backs,

who will probably have children
who will become angry with the town

they live in, the parents
afraid of danger and risk,

those events from the past—
for instance, I could no longer walk

along the top of the stone bridge
above the creek in the town where I grew up,

one leg dangling in the treacherous air
like a clipped bird—

but I remember when I left my own
small place of no consequence,

and now, while we talk
beside a restaurant window,

I suddenly think of that again,
as we toast, our glasses touching,

as those supple, determined boys
spin through the darkness

into their limitless night,
as if what we need to trust, we have.

Early Evening at Marginal Way

Even its name says we have choices that may go wrong.
The sound the wind carries up from the sea
is the voice of what has failed. Although
the tide flattens out along the beach, silent and cold
as glass, small, gray bodies of sparrows
intrude the air, and spray from the rose caps of waves
trails like smoke across the blue/black water,
there is no place for us in any light.
Tonight I will lie without you, all the space
behind the moon and stars unknown, and wonder
how it was we became detached as rain.
Isn't it through natural things our lives seem real?
And aren't the natural acts we deny ourselves
tragedies of spirit? I fear the need
that keeps us distant. I imagine a country
dark enough to touch each other in.

The Gathering

From the porch of this country store,
we watch the Hudson River flow
beside the railroad tracks that stretch
along its bank. An insistent line
of freight cars speeds by and leaves
air, water, light. Here is the sand bar
where Henry Hudson discovered the wet, brown
Iroquois boys and girls, and chose
the name "Kinderhook"—"The Children's Beach."
Now, in a quiet reunion, talk is
of a more recent past, and these summer
fields all of us keep returning to,
while our faces and bodies define
the irretrievable distances between
marriages, divorces, daughters
in college, and half-remembered friendships.
And I am reminded how, in each place
we, like the river, move through ourselves
in some new way. If the world has to end,
it should be at a time such as this:
a cloudless sky, dark slant of wings,
a silence disturbed by the laughter of children.

FROM *MOVIES IN A SMALL TOWN* (1997)

The Commuter

It hardly seems worth it, to live,
I mean, so far away from work.
The woman on the bus sitting
next to me shakes off her sleep.
A man enters his life's equations
onto the eerie green glow
of a laptop computer. Behind me,
another woman talks incessantly
through her phobia of silence.
The driver plays morning news.
I prefer the one most libelous newspaper.
My life then is somehow honest. This week
has been downsizing and a failed deal.
Yesterday, in the office, I swear
I almost wept. At night I screamed
awake from a dream of cats
with horrible human faces. 3:00 a.m.,
our cat was crying for its food.
I don't know why I want it all
to last—this job that has me
traveling sixty miles, my restrained
and modest marriage, the kids' good
grades in school, even the baby's
relentless need. Still,
every day I join the anonymous walk
from one office building to another,
then rise and return from the city's
slow burn and smoke. Lately, I imagine
instead of stopping at our towns,
we keep traveling together until we become
the only world we know, like one of those

lost expeditions of Arctic explorers
who, when discovered after years
of ingenuity and survival, no longer
devour each other from hunger,
but for the ritual.

Lost

You began with death, your mother falling
in her seventh month, so you did not know
your stillborn brother. Your father, who had
your name, and never had enough money,
is now dark. Later, you learned how love dies,
gasping with the best intentions. Never mind
the parents of innocence. This is your room.
They are gone. What if the moonlight that pierces
this window etched you a new name in the shadows,
would the lamps go black, and the street become
loud as memory? You can sleep alone
in a bed in a city where snow piles up
on the flat rooftops until the sun's heat
pushes it off, but you cannot forget. You can
rearrange the books, listen to music, tell yourself
a story, but you will remember when she was
with you. No one knows you, or cares what you've done.
You live in a city where the poor are eating
their shadows, and desire has emptied out the air.
Somewhere, a piano is playing the last long note
of sleep, and you remember. Something you said
made her angry. She turned and left.
You were like a child praying for a way home
through the darkness, promising anything.

Solitude

I walk out to the mailbox and, again, find no news
from you, pull up my collar as a brisk wind approaches,
look across the field, and think of the night we viewed
meteor showers spinning brilliant fires above us.
It was summer, and we were captivated by the sky
as we watched those many flashes swerve along their way.
But this afternoon you are gone, and all the houses nearby
seem to stand and listen in the slowly changing day.
A raccoon scurries toward the path between birch and pine,
then disappears. A jay swells and flutters on a high branch.
I leave the road to go back, instead turn down an incline,
stepping on dried leaves, hard ground and deer tracks.
I remember your hands, hear the road's whispers, bend to where
a sapling is silently reaching into the cold air.

Appearances

Evening, by the window,
as you begin
to turn and sleep,
you are startled by the quick bloom of tulips.

Near the estuary, under the staghorn
branches of sumac,
I watched the dark head of a cormorant erupt,
plunge, then the body rising,
its insistent, blurring flap
lifting it toward afternoon.

The dead lie beneath such noises,
where dogwood petals slip and fall
like a lover's gown.

Florida

Outside the villa, the sky is overcast,
and the dark, rippling pond is laid out
like an enormous thumbprint. Your touch is
a thousand miles away, and here
below the rustling of birds
hidden in the thick desirous leaves of palm trees,
ducks zigzag frantically across the lawn,
compelled, like us, to be somewhere,
then somewhere else.

Tonight I walk to the harbor, where glowing
shrouds of mist hang over the water like lanterns,
and I think of Po Chü-i, who included his poems
in conversation with a woman of his village,
to make certain they were understood.

Why is it so often my life returns to art?
If that ancient Chinese poet were here now,
would he call for the peasant woman who knew poetry,
or simply stroke the hem of his wife's silk robe?

CHLOE'S EPISTEMOLOGY

Bored with the world,
my granddaughter grows restless.
Five months old,
already she wants the grass
to define itself,
the clouded sky
to explain the wind, she wants
the neighbor's barking dog
struggling at the end of a chain
to swallow its vocabulary.

I promise her eternal bloom
of yellow columbine and primrose.
I think she is telling me
to name the world
is only part of that story.
For instance,
say the word "divorce."
Notice its syllables,
how they insist
on remaining together.
I know there is half a century
between us,
and an inexplicable, perpetual
distance. Still,
isn't it truth enough
we are here now,
at the edge of this small,
deathless flowering?

Father's Shirt

I search through the pile of clothes
we tossed off a few hours ago, while my lover
lies in bed. She seems pleased with her sleep,
as if she were quietly drifting past her life.
I dress, the fabric of my shirt flowing
across my shoulders like a cool river,
and remember, as a small child, while
my father slept, finding his unwashed shirt
from the factory with its odors of oil
and grease, the dark stains of what I was told
made things work. Back then I could not imagine
growing into the uniform that had to be worn
in the world of machines and big clocks,
where each day men and women assembled the future.
I wanted to be my father, determined and certain
of what had to be done. I don't know
if I knew we were poor, or why
sometimes Mother cried, or why when Father fished
and we ate, I could taste the river—
its mineral, silt, rock and branch—
even see the place by the stone bridge
where he'd been, afternoon light sparkling
over the water's surface.
I'd plead to go with him next time, and I would.
We were a man and his son, sitting on the bank
beneath a willow tree, waiting together
for the unexpected, and I thought
we'd always return there. Years later,
the day after Father died, and the river seemed still
and empty, I went with Mother
to the town's general store, where she helped me
select a shirt suitable for him to leave in.

Meditations on My Fiftieth Birthday

The eyes, singing like crickets.
The hands, folding their fingers of death.
The head, with its topography of need.

I remember how, in art class,
they taught us to think of the ear
as a question mark,
and spaces between branches were collected
in beautiful, mysterious designs.

So we had created
something detached, outside ourselves,
and the end of life
seemed far beyond the five points
of our crude stars.

I remember how my ear is our universe,
because it too is silence
filled with sound,
and inside each question
is a tightened fist, an imploding wave,
a syncopated drumming
only you can hear.

I Thought of the Clouded, Moonless Night

I thought about arguments
in the clouded, moonless night,
closed around the secret of stars.
I thought about the quivering body,
and the tongue
swelling with reticence,
the eyes aching for sleep.

I thought about summer's end,
of paint that dries
and peels off the side
of an abandoned house.
I thought about my street
that goes into the sea,
and all the fish leaving
the harbor's sick water.

But I am forgetting
my lover, sleepless
and turned
away in our bed, and how
when she leaned toward me
with her white hand,
I was alive
inside her breath.

The River

The overcast sky and gray light seem the same.
I had believed that was the reason I moved
and came back only twice before in twenty years,
each time a funeral—
first Father, then Mother.
What I remember of Main Street is gone
or burned away, and I want to declare,
"This was never my life."
Two o'clock on Monday afternoon,
the church is locked.

The river running through the town
was always lined with willows,
but in their shade its water settles
murky now, and no one fishes.
The renovation of the school,
erected 1919, is a faith
that some things can go on.

All these years, and I was wrong.
The change I'd hoped for
wasn't light.
It was in the sad and empty faces
of Father and my uncle, that year
the rails re-routed
and the factory closed.
The early retirement Father took
brought him an early grave.
That's when the dreams began:
doctor, rain, and priest, the river
flooding, ground too soft
to hold his bones.

At the restored and newly painted home
that once was mine, a child is playing
again on the hill by the elm.
I think of cellar dark, attic heat
and, somewhere in the house,
Mother's troubled call
when she wondered where I'd gone.
Father, I swear the boy will stay
near where you both float, light
as evening air that won't die down.

1948

Everything seemed forever then:
the long, dull day before the bell released
us all from school, the pastor's Sunday sermon,
the high arc of a fly ball, Grandmother's gossip,
my father's sucked-in breath when I'd done something wrong,
a tough kid's punch coming straight at me, a car swerving
toward my big, lumbering dog, and how she stumbled
across the road that morning, to die.

I believed those men in gray wool suits,
and women in floppy, wide-brimmed hats
ornamented with artificial fruit and flowers,
who rushed back and forth in the nineteen-forties
RKO newsreels, bodies jerking like marionettes,
actually moved that way in "real life,"
and imagined my own adulthood, important enough
to have mysterious places I would hurry to.

And I remember clips of beauty queens, generals,
animals made to do strange and funny things,
a pilot leaping from the plane that failed the test,
earthquakes, hurricanes, tornadoes, explosions,
then walking out to the startling afternoon light,
and the small, drab street that would not change,
confused at first by the town's slow motion.

The Note

How many faces have I seen
the moon wear out?
My own face folds and wrinkles
like a well-traveled envelope.

My lover rises from our bed, and enters
into the daily business of dress and work.
In the city, my daughter
offers a breast to her crying infant.

I understand, also, the rows of trees
in the country that fade yearly
away from the poisoned roadside,
and death, their identical complaint.

The Lover

Tonight you come home
from the hospital, tired and cursing
your job, the day, the old woman
who screamed and spit while you knelt,
supplicant as a saint.
I take your feet in my hands.
I do this in memory of snow,
cold winter nights as a child
I came home, my own feet
nearly frozen. And so Mother
would gently rub them,
like a pair of magical lamps
from a storybook—
one wish for the future,
the other for innocence—
rub them back to the purpose of feet,
knowing I would leave again
for the snow forts and ice,
then return like an errant lover
to familiar comfort.
You tilt back your head,
close your eyes to the light,
the bed pans and death,
the pills that won't work.
The dark cathedral of my body
lies next to you.
I doze, and for a moment
smell the elegant wood
of my father's casket, then wake
thinking how our tragic loneliness
is also our magical life.

Movies in a Small Town, 1957

In the dimness, we felt our way along the rows of upholstered seats,
as a pinpoint of light above us suddenly expanded across the screen
like creation. The previews came first, all the best parts
of the future. We watched the show until its final scene,
when the hero we thought was doomed survived after all,
the whole place lit up, and we remembered who we were.

My first job was at that theater, Friday nights,
placing programs for the next week's movies
under the wipers of the parked cars out back.
Once, beneath moonlight and wind flickering through the trees,
a boy's curiosity bent me over the bridge toward a catastrophe
of swirling leaflets, one of those events
that does not seem to be happening to you.
But it was happening to me. Helpless, I saw their lost message
of adventure and romance drop over the dam and disappear.

Past the closed stores and tired faces of shoppers,
I started for home, plotting my explanation. I had learned
how the world could go out of control, and sometimes
we were not what we wanted. I didn't know how this would end.
Outside the taverns, children laughed and played
on the steps, or sat alone in the shadows and cried.
I had no excuse. This was everyone's life.

FROM *SUNDAY EVENING AT THE STARDUST CAFÉ* (2006)

Innocence

I'm dressed inside the family album
for First Communion, pushing my tongue
against the fleshy space where a tooth had been,
and I love Mother and Father, Jesus
and the Blessed Virgin,
a girl in my second grade class
who yells at me for following her.
Look, I'm nearly forgivable
standing under a chorus of angels
in this white suit, even though
once, while reading aloud from *Black Beauty*,
I declared that horse's coat
to be "smooth as Satan,"
and so was held back a year
because, as the nun explained
later to my shamed parents,
I was a strange boy who could not read.

There's a fast-food restaurant
in place of the dining car
where Mother worked, photographs
of it framed in plastic on the wall.
And I remember a trucker
who promised me cowboy boots and hat,
but never drove through town again,
summers on the front porch
watching the Thruway being built,
reports of traffic fatalities
in the local gazette, my father
telling stories to the neighborhood kids,
making each, in turn, a hero,
six-guns drawn, riding a sleek stallion.

I would save us all now, if I could,
from the herd of mistakes
galloping through our hearts.
Once, reshaping our lives
was an easy ritual of customized cars,
rolled-up sleeves, and petroleum jelly.
Then we left town,
or punched in at the factory.
Nothing was simple. No one was blameless.

1954: Two Parades

Just home from Korea, a decorated war hero was leaning
toward the crowd, from the hotel's third floor,
and we heard the drum roll, marching band,
rifle-fire in the humid air, Mother and I,
while Father worked the late shift.

Didn't I know what war was,
times in the weeds I waited for the enemy?
Little Bobby lost an eye in one of those battles,
shot out by his own brother's pellet gun.
I remember, all those childhood years after,
his glass-marble stare seemed wrong,
and his brother's self-hatred.

That was the summer the daughter of the kind woman
who owned the dining car my mother washed dishes in
became Miss New York State, in a parade of lace
and lilacs, their petals the pale lavender
of a heart on the breast of a graceless uniform,
or the satin that ten years later would line my father's casket.
We all stood cheering on the street
to wave along the beauty we were not.

Black Squirrels

(A Gathering of Poets, Kent State University, May, 1990)

Field after field, and gray sky.
Two days on the road, and we're here
for the gathering. After the shootings,
as students drove away from Kent State,
townspeople sat quietly on their porches,
some of them holding rifles.
Back then, like everyone else I knew,
I was going to parties. Once, at one of them,
after I'd taken a hit of blotter acid,
I stared at the bathroom mirror
and it was me all right, only forty years older.
I remember how I went about that evening
with my white hair and beard, my weathered skin,
considerably less astonished by my transformation
than Kafka's Gregor. Our brains were filled
with tiny windows we had to look through.
That's why I was screaming over the bloodied corpse
lying in some Vietnamese field,
or raging against Attica's injustice,
arguing with my parents in the Philco's flickering light.
Everywhere, in May, 1970, the shocked "O"
of that girl on the hill was circling around us.
Twenty years later, poets have come
to read lyrics and remember.
I'm standing next to a grotesque
abstract metal sculpture with a small hole in it,
the scream transfixed, the bullet plummeting
from its high arc above my head.
Black squirrels scurry across the quad.

The poets are still reading, their voices
accumulating into songs, like those
of the bright canaries that, a century ago,
led coal miners who lived here
in and out of their darkness.

Sunday Evening at the Stardust Café

Young people smoke cigarettes,
drink coffee, flirt. A strip of violet
neon tubing thrusts from between the breasts
of Marilyn Monroe in a black and white poster
on the wall. On the jukebox, Neil Young
sings: "Old man, look in my eyes."
Maybe I'll join them, promise to be quick
and reckless. The young blonde
with startling eyes, that seem to reflect
everything, will take me to a quiet booth
in back, where we'll smoke and talk,
as if we're really interested in the bad art
hanging next to us. I can explain then
why my life's important. I remember Marilyn,
her mascaraed, lidded eyes, Presley
censored on Sullivan, Lennon in New York
that night at the Dakota.
Why shouldn't she fall in love?

But I don't want to say too much.
For instance, I can't tell her how sad
the silver-hooped ring dangling from her nose
makes me feel, in spite of my own gold earring.
These kids look like Rimbaud, and far as I know,
they probably are. Think of it, a dozen
reincarnated Rimbauds in a greasy spoon,
pale and dressed in black, notebooks open
to pages ready to record whatever's wrong.

I remember a film, "Wild in the Streets."
The President of the United States,
a rock musician, twenty-five and aging fast,
whose platform was built on the premise
that anyone over twenty-one was suspect,
contemplates his life. In the final frame,
a ten-year-old boy faces the camera
and promises a future of bubble-gum and baseball,
but like with anything else, there's a catch.

Back at the *Stardust*, the waitress,
who is friendly, brings my sandwich.
An old woman mutters, squints at the menu,
and counts her change. Tourists ride
horse-drawn carriages clapping down
the brick streets, or dance on the deck
of a cruise ship entering the harbor.
The kids take their notebooks and leave.

All Our Quick Days

I'm at it again, my old routine
of going places I don't want to be,
because this is what the world
of subways and bank accounts expects.
Overhead, silent messages
of disaster and warning flash
across a computerized screen.
Somewhere in Japan, the car I'm waiting for
was built, the stops I'll make in Boston
recorded in Chicago.
It's no wonder I'm confused.
I tell you, we're not ready for this.
Think about the masturbating monkeys
in a zoo. Years ago, someone homeless
and drunk said to me, "Desire
deferred sickens the heart."
My sick heart trembles now,
and climbs under the artificial suns
of all our quick days.
The purgatory of our troubled sleep
is why I don't take naps.
Instead, I'm sitting with a book open,
pen and paper on the table,
television sound turned off,
not really sure of what I'm doing,
and so look up at the babies being held
underwater by smiling adults
whose heads are nodding in the breathable air,
and although I can't hear an explanation,

I know it has to do with this theory
that fish, frog, infant, and corpse
are all connected,
and it's only time that separates us
from the submerged children.

City That Never Sleeps

> *Chill Wills, a popular character actor during the 1940s and 50s, was the voice of Francis (The Talking Mule), in the Universal Pictures series, and was cast as Chicago, the city itself, in human form in the 1953 film noir classic,* City That Never Sleeps.
> —FROM LEONARD MALTIN'S 2003 MOVIE AND VIDEO GUIDE

Listen. If I can play a talking mule, I can do this. Think about it. How many times did you see me handle Donald, that foolish kid who'd rather dance through the finale than go someplace quiet with the pretty girl who's put up with him the entire movie? Look. Since I was twelve, there's been a red-haired woman dancing inside my head, slowly almost removing the veils shrouding her secret places, but there's always some cop blowing the whistle, and now this: just when the gumshoe who'd been following my every thought was about to quit, he's pulled back in by that dame at the Flamingo, and I can't warn the flatfoot not to leave his wife because the el is rattling the tracks louder than gunfire. But you know how it is, to have your life fast-forwarding like a runaway train; this is just one night, and who wouldn't want a chance to be his own city.

The Question

After the well-broadcast storm,
I went outside with the citizens.
We got in our cars and drove
toward whatever the day would assign.
The sun glared across black ice and snow,
our numbed fingers gripped convenience
store coffee cups, clouded signatures
of breath rising everywhere;
we were bone-chilled and communal.

Listening to "Satisfaction"
 on classic rock radio, I was thinking
about my friend in Florida —
his destroyed orange grove,
how he had learned to love
 the space between things,
and now it was gone —
when a woman stepped out
from behind a parked truck,
her head turned away.
There was nothing to do now
but brake and watch
the woman slide back on her heels,
cars skidding behind me,
an alarm of horns startling
birds off the utility wires.
Then again, we were safe.

Before my friend moved,
we spent a night drinking wine,
It didn't seem like

we'd ever wanted much.
After all, hadn't we come
to accept the mysteries
of cancer and Zen;
wept for the children
gone tragically wrong;
and didn't we still whisper
the names of the saints?

One day you walk out
the door suddenly open
at the middle of your life,
and it's strange to be alone
in the uncertain light,
the question you've been asking
repeating itself, then gone.

Eight Ball

There's a Buddha on my desk,
and he's laughing.
We of the West believe
if you rub the Buddha's belly,
good fortune is certain.
But none of this matters
tonight at the pool hall,
here with a friend —
his shrewd eye and steady hand.
Again, my shot
misses its intention,
and I'm moving inevitably
toward some final chance.

The Buddha was a gift
from my wife.
I believe she meant it
to point out the way
to be different from the self
is to be the self.

For example, the sly
yet generous-hearted manner
with which my friend approaches
the green table and stands,
for a moment,
like a Chinese monk
meditating at the edge
of a quiet field,
is exactly who he is.

He understands
what's important
is more than knowing
what will happen next;
that paying attention
is how we come to the small globe
about to spin away from us,
and call it "safe."

Particular Hearts

> *... Love allows us to walk*
> *in the sweet music of our particular heart.*
> —Jack Gilbert

I walk to the edge of the pier,
where curious tourists point out
a single harbor seal, bobbing and lunging
in the cold winter water,
wet, brown fur slick as sex.
Here is where we've come to be astonished.
"This can't be happening to me,"
we say when things go wrong.
We wonder about the seal,
what it's doing down there,
imagine webbed feet propelling
the impossibly large body
with great speed, toward some inevitable,
glittering fish. This is the chain:
we devour, restore. Today
you and I argued, but when I returned
from seeing all this,
our particular hearts tapped
against a blue door, joined
in the necessary, exquisite surge
toward separate places on our sweat-soaked bedding,
a river of twisted sheets wrapped around our ankles,
our two hearts taking up a constant rhythm
inside their respective rooms.
So many things make us think of our lives.
Isn't that what love is?
Like this morning, in the trees,
when swallows became flash and trill,
and I wanted you here, to listen.

The Station

> *I could not help but cry.*
> *The train, it left the station,*
> *two lights on behind.*
> *Well, the blue light was my blues,*
> *the red light was my mind.*
>
> —ROBERT JOHNSON

And all the sadness you feel
is vibrating in the hands
of the musician by the window,
a line of traffic driving through
the rain-streaked light reflected
in the sheen of his guitar,
and that locomotive, his heart,
traveling farther
than it should have gone,
is suddenly derailed.

Earlier tonight, in a cold rain,
a man sat on the sidewalk
in front of a shop.
You tell the woman
you're with it's all right —
someone will take care of him.

So now the musician is clutching his chest.
His large, gleaming body
staggers and bends forward,
conversations at the tables
fade like the last notes of a song.

The bass player brings him water,
he swallows the pill
he's removed from his pocket,
and it's like everyone
in the room is only alive
to hear him.
The drummer with the snakeskin hatband
lays down his sticks
like a shaman laying down bones,
until the man whose heart
will always hurt can begin again.

Selling the Church

The cold river behind me,
I walked home through a light falling of snow
and epiphany of wind,
past a blessing of Baptist church bells,
and thought how, when I was a boy,
houses of faith seemed eternal
as the soul we children knew
would someday rise from our shocked eyes.
But what did we know then about salvation?
That first year of marriage, I came to understand
my father, who each Sunday knelt in a pew
at Mother's church, although it was a place
he had no faith in. Months later, again
at the church on my street, I'm remembering this
as I read the realtor's sign: "Sale Pending."
Between maple and pine, birds cross
in a religion of weather. What we believe to be true
is what the caretaker raking the leaves
of the minister's yard suddenly says to me:
"Snow tonight. Frost on TV."
It's the gray river and waves against wharf pilings;
the harsh cries of circling gulls and the harbor's silence;
the ritual of a pouring of wine and quiet speech
that is our desire, our prayer.

My Father's Name

Twenty years dead, and still Mother
calls me by his name,
which is a river,
ebb of sea marsh,
mussels and kelp.
It is the lesser heron
and least sandpiper.
It is silt and sea grass,
badger and eel.

Say it again,
it becomes waves
repeating themselves
against the pilings.
It is curve of riverbank.
It is the closed factory
and abandoned houses.
It is a gathering of clouds.

My father's name is a bridge
crossing a river
where a man and son fish
near willows bending
over the murky water
like heads hung in prayer,
and light is a sound
only the dead can hear.

Sunday Factory

We walk the long street
Sunday afternoon,
past the stone church, on our way
to visit his place of work.
This is the religion of father and son,
the faith of a boy who's only five,
the factory a blessing of meat and bread,
the big machines still as statues,
an assembly of clocks
to mark the next week's labor.
Here are the instruments of the makers,
their testaments of gears and wheels.
This is where men and women are called
to the daily stations of common task,
and so I stand with my father
in a child's reverent silence.
Tomorrow, he'll enter the loud,
humming chorus of his eight hour shift
to hose down the conveyor belts
so many times his forearms will ache
until they become light as air.
This is when he thinks of the boy
and his schoolbooks, remembers his wife
and her lilac corsage that morning they married.
And he makes what he can from each of these hours
that will, at last, take him home.

Red Jack

I was twelve that day Father brought me to the home
of his friend, a man living alone, small pension
and afternoons at the window. I remember the percolator's
aroma and dance, a cigar's blue smoke. They sat at the kitchen
table and spoke for a while about the factory closed,
the railroad gone, men they had known lost in the War,
and before that, the Depression and the ten dollar bill
my father left once in his mailbox. And so a boy learned
the tone and gesture of trust and resolve. At my father's wake
seven years later, Red Jack's nephew James stood next to me,
his uncle dead, and we held the silence between us
like a handshake. Once, we had been altar boys,
and served Mass for a priest who kept raising his cup
to the wine cruet, demanding more of Christ's blood,
and when James hid in the sacristy and drank from the rest
until he was sick, I never told. After the funeral, I left town
for college and the decades of mistakes a man can make,
whether he goes away from the place he was born, or not.
James went to work at a local plant, where he lost
two fingers trying to cut metal under a blade
like the older machinists, without using a safety guard.
It was piecework, and he needed the extra money
for the pregnant girlfriend he'd been dating since high school.
They married and, when their two kids had grown
and moved on, divorced. He and I still talk, and last night,
on the phone, it was as if the years of failure, faith, confession,
and hope were being emptied into this single moment,
each of us hanging on to the end of the other's line
and the chance to save ourselves, yet again.

The Train

The train arrives
and birds scatter from the dying elm
to accept the field of late autumn grass.
The land extends a distance
that could reveal
some hidden, unknown thing.
But here, my father, a railroad
man's son, steps across
the rusted, weed-filled tracks,
bringing his suitcase of unspoken words.
In the field, birds forage
insect and seed,
return with cries and questions.
In this dream, I become the ghost
my father was, one man traveling
between small destinations.
He hands me his suitcase,
and waits now as I board the train,
Our face floats through the coach window,
past a sequence of landscapes.
This is America, 1917, the Kaiser "over there";
they've taken German out of the schools,
and I'm left with my one simple language.
It's 1929: Buffalo, New York,
men going over the Falls in a barrel.
I meet a boatman in a bar
the night before a long distance swim
and pay him ten dollars.
Next morning, alone on the gray shore of Lake Ontario,
I decide to go on as far as I can.

Years later, half my stomach gone
to ulcers, I study taxidermy,
and am devoted, for a while, to preserving
the small bodies of frightened animals.
But I get a job, third shift,
cleaning the gelatin-filled machines
at the confectionary dessert plant
next to the railroad tracks, where each night
I listen for the steaming engines.
In 1942, I finally marry. Our first child is stillborn,
and the second so ill the doctors aren't sure
he'll survive, but he does.
Five years old, I baffle the lifeguards
with my determination to remain underwater.
At school, we have air raid drills,
nuns directing us to shelter and prayer.
Sundays, at church, I kneel with my parents
in silence, while songbirds warble in the rafters.
I'm twelve, at the rail yard,
walking the tracks by the coal cars and ash,
kicking gravel into the tunnel's loud darkness.
I can hear a locomotive's whistle,
a diesel's hiss and grind at the crossing,
and Father, we are the trembling earth.

FROM *RADIO TIME* (2011)

Porcelain

Early Saturday afternoon, in winter,
Mother and I are walking
down Elm to the gray and white house
of the Stevens sisters, who were so frail,
I remember, the dust-swirled light
passed through them. "Be careful,"
Mother warned when, in the curiosity
of a four-year-old boy, I picked up
the Boston terrier from the mantel
and turned that tiny figurine
slowly over in my palm. It was then
one of the sisters reached for the collie
and beagle, and when she placed them
on the lace doily draped over the rolled arm
of the button-tufted high back chair,
I saw how the inside of her wrist
had become a small, colorless leaf.

I sat down and soon they were
gathered by me: the Austrian shepherd
and chocolate Siamese, the bulldog
and English setter. And a golden palomino
stood near a grazing brown foal,
while a barn owl, a blue bird,
and a white-throated sparrow
quietly rested. Even the turtle dove
and hummingbird were there, and then
I was raising the birds above my head,
and I sang for them too. And I barked
for the dogs and whinnied for the horses,

and the room filled with flight and the new
sounds I had made for them all,
as those three women watched over me.

Later, while they chatted over tea
and I drank hot cocoa from a thin china cup
painted with tiny roses, snow fell
endlessly outside the frosted window,
and I had held those many things
which I knew now would not break.

Art Lesson

How many times
did I spoon the last taste
of hot fudge from the bottom
and sides of a tulip sundae glass
at Mrs. Ellis's coffee shop,
the portrait she'd painted
of her dead husband,
Gus, no longer dressed
in his white apron, but elegant
now in glowing oils
and dark, vested suit,
hanging above the lunch counter?

She was childless,
hair silver and long,
arranged in a high bouffant,
a portly woman in her sixties,
who only wore purple
or black, and her smile was kind.
All through my childhood,
I brought her my drawings:
crude sketches of houses,
cumulus clouds settling into the low hills,
faces and hands, barns in the fields,
our small town's creek,
the willows that lined its banks—
where boys reckless with summer
dove from a stone bridge—
and the birds that flew over them.

And she'd take me then
to help me make choices
from the glass display case
filled with art supplies:
jars of tempera and tubes of paint,
charcoal and illustration board,
brushes and pastels, tin trays
of bright water colors.

She showed me the imaginary
lines of perspective, how to rub
shadow into light, the proper
placement of eye and ear,
and reminded me often
of the need to erase.
And so I came to learn
both patience and flourish,
and how putting pencil to paper
was just the beginning
of what I might see.

Apples

In October chill the earth-tart scent
of fallen apples brought me to her,
sweet Molly O'Brien, the rich girl
who lived in the white Victorian
with gingerbread trim, largest house
on our street, sprawling front yard
and single apple tree. Those afternoons
I could almost forget how Father returned
each weekday morning covered in factory dust,
Mother steaming in a dining car kitchen.

We were twelve, this good-hearted child and I,
and never spoke about the overdue bills
or grocery credit, the dinner and basket of fruit
the Ladies of Charity delivered to my door one Christmas,
how I hated their cheer and flowered hats.

Many years later, hundreds of miles from that town,
when I went with friends and their children
to pick apples, in that orchard I thought of her again,
as trees yielded what they could no longer bear,
that we might remember kindness.

The Gift of Unwanted Knowledge

Because every evening, ten miles east,
small men guide their nervous horses
to the starting gate, afternoons in our town
my father leans over a pockmarked bar,
checks the history of losses and wins
posted in the latest racing form, collects
the folded slips and wrinkled bills of barroom regulars.

Here, at the dust-twirled Eagle Tavern,
it's 1958, and light glows amber in their glasses
of Pabst Blue Ribbon, Black Label and Genesee.
Where else could faith assemble when the factory's gone,
but in this dark cathedral of last chances? They know
the odds are never with them, but place their bets
like a devoted Sunday congregation.

Outside, the sun is gleaming proudly on the hood
of a new Edsel driving slowly down Main Street.
A few loud boys waving Hubley cap pistols
run from the 5 & Dime, falling then quickly rising
into the repeated resurrection of their play,
as troubled, speechless shoppers step back now,
worried in their sudden search for safety.

And I am one of those running, screaming kids,
toy gun in my hand, freed from school to an afternoon
that needs killing. We had learned what doesn't survive:
Sputnik a cinder descended from the atmosphere
of stars and other planets, Roy Campanella,
once called the best catcher in baseball,
crippled by his car's bad slide and crash.

We heard our fathers, late at night in their darkened houses,
sleepless and bitter, so many things already gone.
We skip flat stones across the surface of the murky creek,
lie shirtless beneath a lowering sun and cool breeze.
If we have questions, they are here in whatever light
is left to hold us, each one his father's son,
and to know what's next is not what we expected.

The Calling

Again the boy calls after the man, and again
I'm walking through memory with my father,
following the trail of theater aisle lights,
down the carpeted path to our seats.
It was 1953, and we'd come to see *Shane*,
and what a nine-year-old might learn
about the friendship of men and clarity of evil.
When I watched Jack Palance, as the hired gun
dressed in black, shoot a stubborn homesteader
and then grin as his body fell
in the mud-filled western street, I knew the name
of all things wrong with the world
was "Wilson." And later, I wondered about the future
of what was right, as a wounded Shane
rode away from that Wyoming valley
and those settlers he'd saved,
the boy Joey hollering for him to come back.
I was too young then to dwell on the enigma
of the woman he could have loved, guess the reason
for the hero's stoic silence, or contemplate
the symbolism of mountains shrouded by clouds.
In the lobby, after the film, I passed a full-length mirror
and imagined, for a moment, who I would become.

Odds Against Tomorrow

Kallett Theater, 1959

Here are three men driving through the fast fall-off
of noir light and shadow, following the Hudson River
toward a small town bank outside Albany
that the disgraced former policeman swears will be an easy score,
and you can tell by the look in their eyes
and grim set of their mouths they need to believe it:
the Harlem musician tired of crooning to the ofay crowd
in smoke-filled bars; the racist war vet, just out of the joint
for hitting a man so hard he killed him but, he reminds his girlfriend,
he didn't mean to do it. Something snapped and he can't remember.
Now they're at a lake's gray shore, close-up
of a half-submerged and ruined china doll, the ex-cop
tossing stones at a crumpled can. In the nearby woods
the veteran points his shotgun at a startled rabbit,
and we have to wonder why he hesitates, until
the frightened animal scurries away, he shoots,
and then we understand. Of course, the robbery goes wrong.
We already knew this plan wouldn't work: the ex-cop dead in an alley,
the musician and veteran running past the rail yard into the looming
rows of oil terminals, and a confrontation that had to happen.
But it's what the camera shows us next that makes us
sit up straight. In a scene reminiscent of Cagney's finish
in *White Heat*, they climb on top a tank and fire simultaneously
at each other, the screen exploding in flame and rising smoke,
in the aftermath, their scorched bodies laid side by side.
And in this time out of time we know failure,
desperation, even greed, each of us unrecognizable
in the darkened theater of our collective breath:

student and teacher; housewife and sales clerk;
grocer and mechanic; the teenage couple
necking in the last row. And "Who,"
the first detective to arrive is asking,
"can tell the difference?"

Our Fathers' Clothes

And so now we wanted other lives,
sixteen-years-old on a summer evening,
coming out of the small town's theater
after *Dr. No* —Ursula Andress in a bikini,
suddenly emerging on a white Jamaican beach,
suntanned and rapt with private song;
Connery as Bond, dark browed and sexual,
stepping out from behind a dune, singing back.
And later, in a perfect tuxedo, Bond wins
at roulette, and deftly places a chip
in the cleavage of that night's good fortune.
These were not our fathers' clothes—
 those men of field and factory labor,
Friday's poker ante, Schaefer beer,
 a cigar's reward, gabardine trousers,
and rolled up sleeves. But when we stopped
at the Hickey-Freeman men's store
 window, our reflected images
 dissolved the manikins' blank stares,
until we boys became the characters
in a movie of our own making, confident as men
dressed in slightly tilted fedoras, carefully peaked
handkerchiefs pointing out the breast pockets
of our blended wool, three-button coats,
jacquard print ties in Windsor knots
on Hathaway shirts, the cuffs of pleated pants
just breaking over polished oxfords.
Then a fade to the final scene:
we walked home through the dimly-lit streets—
our fathers' sons.

Radio Time

> *Is low the moon, but high the wind*
> —CHUCK BERRY

A howling dog, transistor radio crackling,
Chuck Berry: cars, girls and school,
and there, from the nightstand in my bedroom,
something close to revelation.
Ex-con—Kansas City joyride, broken down
car and jail, yet this skinny black man
and his guitar knew how to be sixteen.

And here, too, the gravelly voice
of George "Hound Dog" Lorenz,
who each evening on WKBW—"the greatest
station on your dial"—proclaimed
"The Hound's Around," and reminded us listeners
if we were "hangin" around the corner,"
we were "doggin' it." And I was transfixed

as that DJ spun those forbidden records
through the airwaves: Fats Domino,
LaVern Baker, The Moonglows, The Five Satins,
Ann Cole, Joe Turner, The Clovers,
Little Richard & The Upsetters, Etta James
lamenting "All I Could Do Was Cry."

And so it was I came to hear again
those historians of desire, prophets
of a change that would soon be mine.

The Other Language

Even her worried voice couldn't bring me
to answer the morning I hid in weeds
by the willow, some child's wrong idea
of his importance in the known and safe world.

Or perhaps it was a simple insistence
that my life mattered, that Mother would,
if I were really gone, after all miss her only son,
and regret those scoldings and rules.

But I came then to understand silence's bitter ache:
Mother turned away at the kitchen stove,
her darkened thoughts of a cold river
and drowned boy shadowing the sun-filled wall.

When Barbara Jean stepped from the line
of high school cheerleaders and leapt
into the brisk October air, calling out each letter
of my name, I ran gladly with the others
onto the field of end runs and tackles.

But what was announced over the PA that afternoon
we stood assembled at the gymnasium rally,
navy blazers and striped ties, our season's ritual
of recognition and awards: the President
shot and yes, dead, startled everyone quiet,
and then so strangely alone.

Once, I watched my father and his deaf mute friend
speak in the quick conversation of hand and fingers,
saw how it was we might become our own words,
and for years after Father died there were nights
I dreamt back his voice, but woke to my loud cries.

At Sunday Mass with my parents, I had believed
those mysterious Latin chants would save me,
held as certain scripture the impossible
stories of a favorite uncle, learned the lessons
of home and school, and listened for the truth,
as I do still, of who we are that has not been said.

The Industrial Diamonds of 1964

That spring I dropped out of college
and took a factory job back in the small town
I had been so certain I'd never return to,
and stood at my task of gears and wheels,
where I cursed—or it could have been prayer—
through each shift's final hour.

In the lunch room, old-timers
mocked the new hires, argued
about Kennedy, Oswald, and Ruby,
and how those damn Cubans were
behind it all. That was why we had
to stay in Vietnam, and to hell
with the hippies and Commies.

We were grinding circular saw blades,
fitting them with industrial diamonds,
and each hundred-thousandth inch meant
a paycheck we might live with, something
to take every Friday to the bank and tavern,
place of dimmed lights, twenty-five cent draughts,
baseball scores, boxing matches,
horse racing odds, the two-dollar-bet,
and a chance few of us believed in.

I think of those men now, and remember
our labor, the metal shavings I washed off
my hands and arms each night at the sink,
the ache of shoulders and wrists, the blessing
of sleep, the pre-dawn wakening to rock and roll
music playing on the clock radio,
the gem-like glitter of a few last stars,
and then the turbulent and risen sun.

The Annual Richard Milhous Nixon Pig Roast & 4th of July Celebration

Each year we gathered at the summer field
in Eastern New York, the Berkshires rising above
hemlock ravines. We came because we had survived
a decade of Vietnam, Watergate and White House scandals,
riots that had turned whole city blocks to smoldering despair.
And still we danced, rock music then our true religion
in the collective spirit of half-naked bodies and chemical haze,
or we circled, like a tribe, around the roasting animal.

But some nights I wandered out into the crepuscular flash
of lightning bugs, those mythic lanterns of the meadow,
listening, for a while, to a chorus of crickets, and the soft voices
inside tents pitched on the low hills nearby, murmuring toward sleep.
O brothers and sisters, how those years we loved the natural world,
and too all the rituals and totems of a changed empire.

Once, I stood with a friend on one of those hills after a rain,
and the sky, I swear, opened itself green, while a woman in the valley
below lifted off her cotton print dress with an almost paradisaical grace,
and danced there in the yellow clover and honeysuckle,
ecstatic and glorious now in the unimpeachable new light.

At the Currier Gallery of Art

Giovanni Battista Tiepolo, "Triumph of Hercules"
(modello for a fresco ceiling, c. 1761)

Hercules is pulled from his funeral pyre.
Spirited horses drive his chariot.
Winged gods with trumpets
rise from their beds of clouds.

I imagine Tiepolo's assistants
on their scaffolds, their labor of design,
their master observing
the scene's exuberant formation—

stone and wings,
man-god and his retinue,
emblazoned light above the dome
of that palace in Verona.

A placard reveals what's here
is the hysterical sadness of art.
This painting's a "modello."
Here's an explanation of the bombing:

World War II. Palazzo Canossa destroyed.
The fresco ceiling shattered.
I'm beneath it all, nearly weeping now,
in spite of what's been saved.

Everywhere Is Everywhere

These days, words from the gospels
and old hymns are rolled out on screens
across eternal Midwestern sky.
Somewhere, between Iowa City
and Cedar Rapids, driving along
miles of nearly vacant road,
past cornfields that once were ocean,
rows of glittering pumpkins,
and Amish farmers riding their slow carriages,
my friend and I are discussing
transcendental meditation and Dutch women,
high school football and local politics,
the recently sanctioned shooting
of overpopulated deer, with bow and arrow.

I look out as a flock of finches
rises and falls in thermals of blue air,
then rises again high above the bowed heads of cattle
grazing in an open field edged with hay bales,
and the offering of road before us
repeats itself like some chant
from a prayer that would take us home forever.

Against Happiness

When the Dalai Lama first heard
the bombs falling on Tibet,
he whispered to a monk,
"They have stolen our silence."

Today, at the clinic,
again the loud radiation machine
whirred above my head.

But later, my doctor,
who is beautiful,
placed her delicate fingers
around my throat,
like so many butterfly wings.

I knew then it was time
to abandon my elaborate theories
of happiness and to be,
instead, the butterfly.

What to Say If the Birds Ask

And if clouds gather now like distant cousins,
it's because weather is the mother of all things
cyclical. And if, through the afternoon rain,
the mail carrier comes with her armful of bills
and rejection, it's only to remind us of what
we may have yet to receive. But what unsettles
me this gray morning beneath trill and chatter of birds,
signals of a coming storm in a neighborhood of strangers,
is that first death, polished wood and Uncle's cold hand
when I was nine, the relatives and friends gone since then,
my futile guilt and anger, the failed language of regret.
But if it's true some words are, finally, the soul's
lexicon, then I'll say this: Once, there was a woman
whose shadow blessed the light of a room in Boston,
a man who filled the glasses of his friends with the best wine,
a child who tasted the soft petals of flowers and spoke
their many colors to swans rippling the summer pond
in a silent lyric. Today, alone by the window, I've been
translating the repeated warble of sparrows perched
on the maple's high branches. "What's next? What's next?"
they ask. "Soon," I whisper, "Soon, we will know."

The Garden

In his garden, my friend
has become adept
at mimicking the birds
as now, through the night's
wet veil, he repeats
their many songs,
until even the prolific
mockingbird must listen.
A curious gecko hangs,
for a moment, over the top
of the porch screen,
then scurries into the shadows.

We've been sitting for hours
with drink and conversation.
I've just traveled
the Atlantic coast to be here,
and am thinking now
of that wise poet, Po Chü-i,
how he believed in seclusion
and clarity, yet sometimes
welcomed visitors, and once wrote:
Who says the moon is heartless?
It's followed me a thousand miles.

Tomorrow, we'll wake
as the red-eyed Cooper's hawk
rises above the blossoming
purple bougainvillea,
waving banana leaves,
that extravagant bird
of paradise, and the mango
trees heavy with fruit
nearly touching the ground.

Thrush & Squirrel

Suddenly a squirrel scampers along the edge
of the tall wooden fence, a hermit thrush,
high pitched, in pursuit, and you laugh
because it seems like such play,
but at stake are the eggs in their cup
of moss, leaves, and rootlets, the four flutes
you might never hear silent now inside
the thin walls of their shells. And you
understand why this must be your life,
the melodious song you wait for certain
to flicker, after all, through the absence
your body will one day become.

NEW POEMS

Absence & Event

Because you are gone
for a week, and I don't
want to consider loneliness,
I go out to the garden
and water the red roses
that have climbed
up the white lattice
trellises and now probe
through the small,
open squares of their windows,
like the bright faces
of curious children.

Back in the house,
I quiet the need of our two cats
with a bowl of dry food.
I make coffee and,
for a while, read the newspaper
with its reports of war,
accidents, town politics,
and sad photographs
of the dead and arrested.

If you were here,
I might ask that we walk
together to the river,
where ubiquitous gulls
circle above the abandoned
mills and current's gray flow,
a few locals fishing,

and the occasional ducks
scrambling onto shore.
But this afternoon
I'm alone at my desk,
where I'm writing
about the day's simple events—

and you are the space
between each necessary word.

Wonder

> *Wonder and desire are how the self changes*
> *into the camouflage of everything.*
> — JACK MYERS

And so it is these unhidden wrens cry their high pitches
from the stark branches of a winter maple.

Even if I did revisit the past,
what could I change that wouldn't unravel
the cloth of who I need to be?

When, before the bells of wisdom and compassion chimed,
Buddha was asked why there was no self,
his answer disappeared into silence.

If I were to speak out now,
the one who would listen is gone,
and the self I am not is the sound of an echo
after the bells have been struck.

At The Wilkes-Barre/Scranton Airport Meditation Room

A quiet hour in the votive light
of the airport's meditation room,
I'm left to reflect on the good nature
of friends and the comfort of their stone house
and walks along the river, and now these passages
of divinity and speculation bound in testaments
neatly arranged by design, not doctrine.
What words might save me, in the time that's left
before I'm lifted above rain and thunderous predictions
of the world's religions? It's true, I believe I'll arrive,
everything just as I left it, and yes, it's also true I can't
give up those mistakes I might never get to make.
But there's proof the spirit sustains us; just listen
to those jazz compositions by Parker and Coltrane
we heard last night, while we sat smoking on the porch
of the Deer Head Inn, the noisy chatter of tourists
receding beneath an improvised flurry of melody and dissonance.
Consider yesterday afternoon and the faith of those boys
at Bushkill Falls, sliding down cascades into one pool after another,
like these passengers and I who wait to depart
in unnatural flight toward our separate destinations.

Brotherhood

No matter now, he died before his name
and lies in an unmarked grave, Father the only one
to see the shriveled blue/gray boy lost that August
afternoon at the corner of Clay and Myrtle,
Mother slipping on a step, something loosened
and horribly wrong, weeks later, the child stillborn.
How do we speak for the missing breath,
call after the silence of one who is gone?

Summer evenings, a child at the creek bank,
I was the early cricket in an unseen world.
Those years I imagined him, the older brother,
the shade that followed me down
the tree-lined streets of my small town life.
I had been born from death into the world's mysteries
punctuated by barking dogs, Sunday dinners,
the many demands on a boy at play, and a past
somehow at once finite and eternal.

Ash

Friends gather in their groups of memory
and celebrate the bodiless click and song
of a darkened wood, the restored house
with its three windows edged by blue,
red and crystalline squares of stained glass,
the raised arms of a green ceramic Buddha,
think also of those lost years, a woman
in a predawn acid high running in rain
through the city's cobblestone streets, her long cape
flapping like the wings of some flightless bird,
moonlight and a barroom's neon glare
across the hood of a white '55 Ford in summer,
a 1930s Buck Roger's poster and a question:
"Is this man really 2,000 years ahead of his time?"
and that Z.Z. Hill lyric: "Woo Wee Bop!
Baby I'd chop / off my right arm for your love."
Now children of the father who last week became ash
sit together in their loud silence, the widow
quietly folds her hands, someone delivers trays of food
and places them on tables draped in white cloth,
then it's my turn to speak. I know nothing of death,
but I remember once, having been called
by the quick signatures of lightning bugs,
his small daughter brought me to an open field,
where she discovered her name among a constellation of stars.

Who Can Say?

When the boatman never arrived,
my father swam the long distance meet
as far as he could before
climbing into someone else's boat,
exhausted, yet redeemed.

Mother wanted me to join
the priesthood,
but Sharon Murphy's blue eyes
and long blonde hair
were more glorious
than any sacrament.

Those early autumn days
during recess in the schoolyard—
a reprieve from the rooms of ink wells,
catechisms and wooden rulers—
we boys died and were resurrected
in our games of war.

Sometimes now I read
the evening paper,
tune into the 6 o'clock report,
all for the sake of learning
any news
that isn't mine to bear,
then I sit watching
late night TV, enveloped
by flickering shadows
of film noir want.

Who can speak of loss,
say what it is anyone needs
as those winter birds
call out the names for wind?

Mise-En-Scène

The Isles of Shoals, Star Island

Water speaks a film noir at the shoreline
this afternoon in island light,
the shimmering ocean pure cinema,
at once dark and luminescent,
like those 1940s movies
of mood and singularity,
and standing at the dock,
I think I understand the loneliness
of Bogart or Mitchum
as they search for clues
that might solve the mystery,
but already know things will never be right
between them and the women they have to follow.
So in a scene bursting with gunfire,
when the wounded PI falls out of the crashed Buick,
you hope, beyond hope really, he's survived.
And isn't it fitting that such tragedy
be expressed in black and white, underscored
by those ambiguous shades of gray —
the beauty we want, the life we think we need?
Meanwhile, in *Algiers*, Charles Boyer
as "Pepe," a master thief, looks into the eyes
of Hedy Lamarr, the bejeweled and beautiful "Gaby,"
sitting across from him at the café
(she's all glimmer and gloss)
and quietly asks: "Who were you before the pearls?"
And I'm reminded of that homeless guy
in Albany, years ago, who warned me:
"Desire deferred sickens the heart."

Perhaps that's what our anti-hero means
when he tells the femme fatale: "You're like a leaf
the wind blows from one gutter to another."
But here the wind echoes azure
against the wharf pilings, all the wrong words
returned and changed as waves.

The Past

I've returned to the street and small hill,
the house where outside the boy still runs through the yard,
a child who has yet to learn shame and poverty's rage,
who reinvents his dead brother in games of war and perfect victory,
who doesn't hear the whispered names of the lost
until they drift into the storied song of birds filling the aged elm.

The boy's father watches from the kitchen window,
two hours before his wife, a dining car waitress, will come home
and then his shift at the factory next to the railroad tracks, whistle blasts,
and diesel locomotives pulling long lines of trembling freight cars
through the dark tunnel of his troubled thoughts, toward the next paycheck
he knows won't be enough, but just now, here is his son.

There are summer evenings after a rain, by that patch of lilies-of-the-valley
where they buried the family dog last spring, father and son
bring shovel and coffee can to dig for night crawlers, and a morning
of fishing at the creek bank, when they'll sit by a willow,
talk about school and baseball, what the boy imagines of his life
after this town that grows smaller every year, all those Sundays and Latin chants.

I've been back twice since Father died, Mother's funeral and this visit
to the house restored and unrecognizable in its fresh paint under new shingles,
but I can hear the voices of children on the front porch counting cars driving past,
then there's a sudden quiet to the afternoon and I have learned a prayer
for the bright tulips Mother planted, that rose up each April like hands
waving in praise of what was greater than ourselves.

NOTES

"The Balance" is for James DeCrescentis. "Martin's Nursing Home," "The Question," "The Garden," and "Thrush & Squirrel" are for William Kemmett. "From the Cabin at Otter Lake" is for Lynnie Boyce. "Remembering What Was Said," "Anatomy Lesson," "The Canal," and "How We Pray" are for Amy Brand. "Day Labor" is for James Haug. "The Vacant Lot on Jefferson Avenue," "The Gathering," "The Annual Richard Milhous Nixon Pig Roast & 4th of July Celebration," and "Ash" are for Keith A. Kuzmak. "Chloe's Epistemology" is for Chloe Edwards. "Eight Ball" and "Wonder" are for Jack Myers. "Black Squirrels" is for Peter Kidd and Richard Blevins. "The Station" is for the Mississippi delta blues musician Big Jack Johnson. "The Gift of Unwanted Knowledge" is for Al Maginnes. "Odds Against Tomorrow" is for Tom Absher. "Radio Time" is for Al Peterson. "Everywhere is Everywhere" is for Rustin Larson. "Absence & Event" is for S Stephanie. "At the Wilkes-Barre/Scranton Airport Meditation Room" is for Jim and Linda Elsaesser.

ACKNOWLEDGMENTS

Grateful acknowledgment is made to the following publications, where many of the poems in this collection previously appeared, sometimes in different versions:

Anabasis: "Early Evening at Marginal Way"; "The Gathering"

The Anthology of New England Writers, 1995: "In the Woods at Hills Acres"

The Aurora: "Eight Ball"; "My Father's Name"

Baybury Review: "Florida"; "Lost"

Berkeley Poetry Review: "The Balance"; "What We Did Wrong, 1956"

Birmingham Poetry Review: "Murder at Jug City"

The Café Review: "Anatomy Lesson"; "The Commuter"

Calliope: "Innocence"; "Movies in a Small Town, 1957"; "1954: Two Parades"; "The Note"

Cider Press Review: "All Our Quick Days"; "The Calling"; "Everywhere is Everywhere"

Cimarron Review: "Chloe's Epistemology"

Cincinnati Poetry Review: "From the Cabin at Otter Lake"

Connotation Press: An Online Artifact: "The Gift of Unwanted Knowledge"; "Odds Against Tomorrow"; "The Other Language"

The Contemporary Review: "Black Squirrels"; "Selling the Church"; "The Station"

Country Journal: "Silver Lake"

Defined Providence: "1948"; "Meditation on My Fiftieth Birthday"; "Particular Hearts"

Drunken Boat: "Wonder"

The Eleventh Muse: "Desire"; "First Catch"

Embers: "Poem For Richard Hugo"

Fell Swoop: "The Funeral"

The Fourth River: "Thrush & Squirrel"

Gargoyle: "The Last Hold"

Mid-American Review: "The Canal"; "Day Labor"; "Sunday Evening at the Stardust Café"

Poet & Critic: "Remembering What Was Said"

Poet Lore: "Father's Shirt"; "Martin's Nursing Home"

Poetry East: "Against Happiness"; "The Annual Richard Milhous Nixon Pig Roast & 4th of July Celebration"; "Art Lesson"

Saranac Review: "Apples"; "Consideration"; "Radio Time"

The Tower Journal: "Ash"; "Porcelain"

Tygerburning: "At the Wilkes-Barre/Scranton Airport Mediation Room"; "Mise-en-scène"; "The Past"

White Pelican Review: "What to Say if the Birds Ask"

The Vermont Literary Review: "Absence & Event"

"Martin's Nursing Home" was reprinted in *Open Door: A Poet Lore Anthology 1980—1996* (Writer's Center Editions, 1997)

"1948" was reprinted in the *1997 Anthology of Magazine Verse & Yearbook of American Poetry* (Monitor Books)

"Red Jack" and "Sunday Factory" were reprinted in *Leaves by Night, Flowers by Day* (1st World Publishing, 2006)

"Eight Ball" was reprinted in *The Café Review* (special tribute issue to Jack Myers, 2010).

"Ash" and "Porcelain" were reprinted in *An Endless Skyway: Poetry from the State Poets Laureate* (Ice Cube Press, 2011).

Poems in this book have been selected from *The Required Dance* (Igneus Press, 1990), *Movies in a Small Town* (Mellen Poetry Press, 1997), *Sunday Evening at the Stardust Café* (1st World Publishing, 2006), and *Radio Time* (Cherry Grove Collections, 2011).

Several of these poems also appeared in the chapbooks *The Inheritance* (Four Zoas Press, 1983), *A Season of Crows* (Igneus Press, 2000), *White Bees* (Oyster River Press, 2001), *Sunday Factory* (Finishing Line Press, 2006), and *What to Say if the Birds Ask* (Pudding House, 2007).

For their many years of friendship and support, I wish to express my gratitude to Peter Kidd, editor/publisher of Igneus Press, James DeCrescentis, James Duffy, David Allan Evans, Glenn J. Freeman, James Haug, Al Maginnes, and Richard Martin.

Thanks to Mark DeCarteret for encouraging me to compile this collection, and for his careful reading and good advice. Thanks also to Rustin Larson, William Kemmett, and S Stephanie for their suggestions on poems to include, and to *Hobblebush* editors Sid Hall and Rodger Martin for their enthusiastic support and editorial guidance.

ABOUT THE AUTHOR

W. E. BUTTS is the author of four previous books of poetry, including *Radio Time* (Cherry Grove Collections), named poetry winner at the 2011 New England Book Festival, and *Sunday Evening at the Stardust Café*, which was chosen as a finalist for the 2005 Philip Levine Prize in Poetry from the University of California/Fresno and selected winner of the 2006 Iowa Source Poetry Book Prize, and he has published several chapbooks. His poems appear frequently in such journals as *Atlanta Review, Birmingham Poetry Review, Cimarron Review, Mid-American Review,* and *Poetry East*, and have been reprinted in many anthologies, including *An Endless Skyway: Poetry from the State Poets Laureate* (Ice Cube Press, 2011). The recipient of two Pushcart Prize nominations and a Massachusetts Artists' Foundation Award, he is the 2009–2014 New Hampshire Poet Laureate, and teaches in the low-residency BFA in Creative Writing Program at Goddard College. He lives in Manchester, New Hampshire with his wife, the poet S Stephanie.

THE HOBBLEBUSH GRANITE STATE POETRY SERIES

HOBBLEBUSH BOOKS publishes several New Hampshire poets each year, poets whose work has already received recognition but deserves to be more widely known. The editors are Sidney Hall Jr. and Rodger Martin. For more information, visit the Hobblebush website: *www.hobblebush.com*.